Come Write With Me:

POETRY

Workbook & Journal

Brooke E. Wayne

For
TWEENS
& YOUNG
TEENS
Volume 1

Hearts & Flowers
Publishing

Contact the author at www.brookeewayne.com, "Contact Me".

ISBN-13: 978-1-7341637-1-1
ISBN-10: 1-7341637-1-1

Chief Editor: Anette Blaskovich

Title: Come Write with Me: POETRY Workbook & Journal (For Tweens & Young Teens)
Author: Brooke E. Wayne
Publisher: Hearts & Flowers Publishing
Excerpts: Public Domain
Cover Photo: Shuttershock
Font: American Typewriter
Graphics: Pixabay.com, PublicDomainVectors.com (Free Stock Photos for Publication)

Description: A workbook loaded with creative writing tools to compose poetry, including fill-ins, worksheets, examples, structured writing exercises, unstructured journal space, and much more!

Category: Creative Writing Workbook, Creative Writing Journal, Poetry Workbook, Poetry Journal, Creative Writing Prompts, Poetry Writing Prompts, Poetry Starters, Creative Writing Starters, Poetry Lessons, Creative Writing Lessons, Structured Creative Writing, Instructional Workbook, Poetry Curriculum, Poetry Lessons, Middle Grade Poetry

A Special Thank You to...

Anette Blaskovich for your eagle-eye editing skills and amazing perception. Thank you for always thinking outside the box with my work and helping me truly see where I am only looking.

TABLE OF CONTENTS

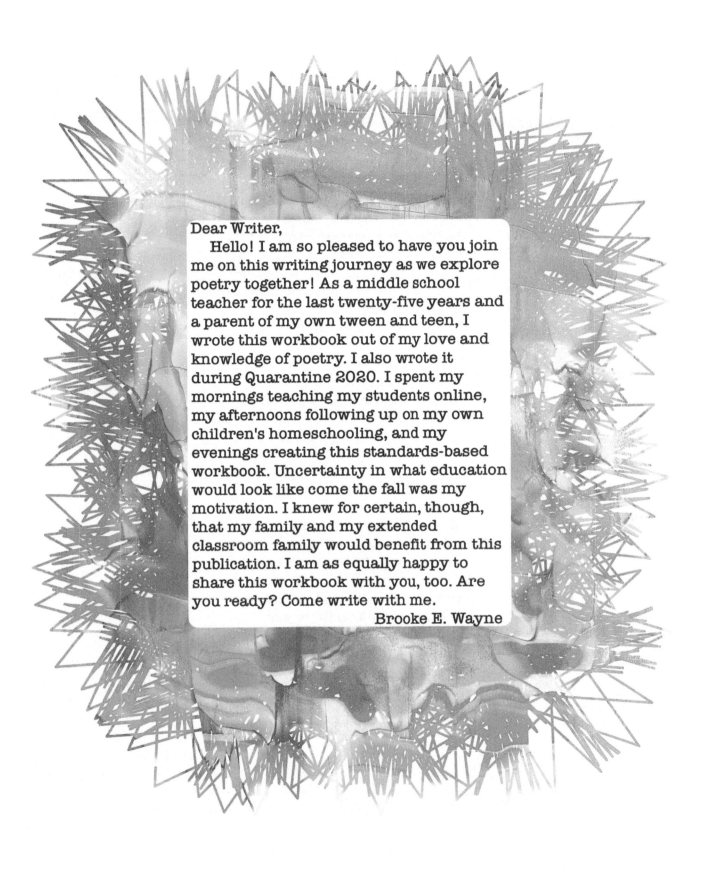

Dear Writer,

Hello! I am so pleased to have you join me on this writing journey as we explore poetry together! As a middle school teacher for the last twenty-five years and a parent of my own tween and teen, I wrote this workbook out of my love and knowledge of poetry. I also wrote it during Quarantine 2020. I spent my mornings teaching my students online, my afternoons following up on my own children's homeschooling, and my evenings creating this standards-based workbook. Uncertainty in what education would look like come the fall was my motivation. I knew for certain, though, that my family and my extended classroom family would benefit from this publication. I am as equally happy to share this workbook with you, too. Are you ready? Come write with me.

Brooke E. Wayne

HOW TO USE THIS BOOK

Every poet is a unique individual,
bringing one's own special talents
to his or her creative writing.
My hope is that this workbook and journal
enables you to grow as a writer
through the exercises and insights I have put into
Come Write with Me:
Poetry Workbook & Journal
(For Tweens & Teens).
You will start with polishing up your skills
at writing poetic devices
and putting them into practice.
Then, feel free to bounce around in this book.
You can flip to the back
and write some Structured Poetry,
or you can move forward, page by page,
and dabble in some Imagery,
or even hop around the variety of
Prompts you'll find tucked in the middle.
Be sure to review the Literary Terms
and handful of Grammar Terms
before the Poetic Devices, though,
so you will be able to understand
the letters I write to you
throughout your journey
in writing poetry with me.

Creative Writing
Toolbox

Hey, Psst! I want you to think of
Figurative Language
as a big bag of tricks.
Inside this bag are all kinds of writing
techniques--the tricks--that make
writing go from snooze-fest to fabulous.
These tricks are not only called
Figurative Language collectively,
but they are often referred to as
Poetic Devices, too.
We will be exploring a handful of these
creative writing tricks in the next section.
I highlight each Poetic Device
with a definition, an example of it
in action in a classic poem,
and offer several prompts
to help you get started.
My goal is to get you so used to
snatching one of these tricks
out of your mental bag
of Figurative Language
that you automatically add
them to your poetry because
it doesn't feel right if you don't.

PARTS OF SPEECH

I don't know about you, but grammar makes me all cringy.
Doing grammar right when we're writing is one thing,
but knowing the formal terms of the parts that we're doing
is a whole other matter.
The thing is, though, understanding these terms
makes completing a few of the sections in this workbook,
where I happen to reference them,
easier and more user-friendly.
Same goes for the Literary Terms on the following page.
So study-up, buttercup.

NOUN-----A person, place, or thing, or idea--like freedom

VERB-----An action, state of being, or condition

ADJECTIVE-----A descriptive word

PREFIX-----A word part that is added to the beginning of a base word to alter its meaning

SUFFIX-----A word part that is added to the end of a base word to alter its meaning

PRESENT PARTICIPLE-----A form of a verb that sometimes functions like an adjective.
It is created by adding the suffix "ing" to the base word. Present-tense puts the action of the
descriptor happening in the moment

LITERARY TERMS

END RHYME-----The ends of two or more lines of poetry rhyme together

FREE VERSE-----A poem that cannot rhyme

FOOT-----A measurement of stressed and unstressed syllables (Syllables are pronounciated word parts: beau-ti-ful has three syllables)

INTERNAL RHYME-----A line of poetry that rhymes in the middle and end of the same line

LYRIC-----A highly musical poem, conveying powerful feelings or glimpsing only a portion of a story

METER-----Counting accented and unaccented syllables in a word or group of words, measured by metrical feet (iamb, trochee, spondee, dactyl, anapest)

NARRATIVE POEM-----A poem that reflects a complete story with a beginning, inciting moment, middle, and end that satisfies the reader (may or may not rhyme)

POETIC DEVICES-----Figurative language used to enhance a poem

POINT OF VIEW (POV)-----Perspective or voice a story is told from (1st POV--I, my, me... 2nd POV--you ... 3rd POV--he, she, they ...)

RHYME SCHEME-----Alphabetically labeling the end rhymes of a poem, creating a pattern (Example: ABAB CDCD EFEF GG)

RHYTHM-----A pattern of stressed and unstressed beats composed of metrical units

STANZA-----A group of lines in a poem--the way essays have paragraphs, poems have stanzas

SIMILE

When two uncommon items are compared to each other, often using like or as.

A Red, Red Rose

"Oh, my Luve is like a red, red rose,
That's newly sprung in June;
Oh, my Luve is like the melody
That's sweetly played in tune."
(Excerpt)

by
Robert Burns

On the following page, you will see a brainstorming box with several prompts for you to use, tweak into something better, or ignore, if you want to. Fill the blank lines with your own ideas, too.

Dear Writer,

As you can see in Burns' poem, Luve, which is an old-timey way of saying Love, is being compared to a rose during springtime, and then again as the melody in a song.

A simile, as one of your "tricks", has a unique way of turning two different items into best buds with all kinds of creative things in common even though, at first, the items might seem more like arch enemies. (See what I did there with, "items like...enemies"? Anyone? Anyone?)

To help you remember this device, I want you to think about similes as being similar-- not because the two items actually have anything at all to do with each other, but because they've found a way to hang out together anyway.

Similes enhance the way the poem makes the person feel because of the association of things. For an added challenge, I want you to find a comical way to use a simile in your creative writing.
You've got this!

~Brooke E. Wayne

joyful like/as a bouquet of balloons
smile like/as a ray of sunshine
lumpy like/as a sack of marbles
laughter like/as a warm blanket
creepy like/as carnival clowns
cold like/as a cube of ice
sing like/as an angel's sigh
fear like/as a dark alley
silky like/as a satin ribbon
scream like/as a blaring siren
pain like a pinch to the skin
peaceful like/as snowfall in winter
happy like/as a litter of wiggly puppies

_____
_____
_____
_____
_____
_____
_____
_____
_____
_____

Example:
The <u>players</u> walked onto the grass <u>like tigers</u> on the prowl, scanning their prey on the other side of the field as their opponents stretched before the big game.

_____

_____

_____

_____

_____

_____

_____

_____

_____

_____

_____

_____

_____

_____

_____

_____

_____

_____

_____

_____

_____

_____

_____

_____

_____

_____

_____

_____

_____

_____

_____

_____

_____

_____

_____

_____

_____

_____

_____

_____

_____

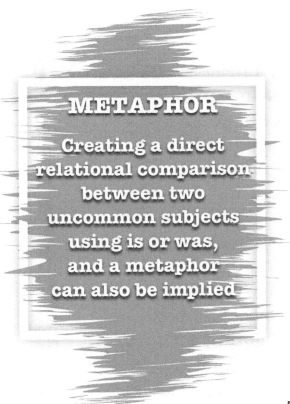

METAPHOR

Creating a direct relational comparison between two uncommon subjects using is or was, and a metaphor can also be implied

Text

'"Hope" is the thing with feathers"

'"Hope" is the thing with feathers–
That perches in the soul–
And sings the tune without the words–
And never stops–at all–"
(Excerpt)

by
Emily Dickinson

On the following page, you will see a brainstorming box with several prompts for you to use, tweak into something better, or ignore, if you want to. Fill the blank lines with your own ideas, too.

Dear Writer,

Emily Dickinson was an American poet who lived during the 1800s. Everyone in town thought she was a weirdo because she wore 'odd' clothes that didn't conform to society's fashionable standards, she hardly ever left her bedroom, let alone her house, and she wouldn't talk to anybody unless it was through written notes.

Nowadays, these habits would make her a typical teen holed up in her bedroom with her nose buried in texts. Am I right? Turns out, though, Dickinson, the quirky introvert, was a secret poet. After she died, her family found over 1800 poems in her bedroom, and, of course, they published them!

Many of her sweet poems are hysterical--wrought with wit and pith--and loaded with sarcastic or beautiful comparisons. Her writing tends to drip with deep messages, too, like the example shown that centers on "hope" as a bird.

A metaphor is a powerful poetic device that forces the reader to accept the association of two dissimilar objects by flat-out saying one thing 'is' another.

Yeah, hanging out in my room writing creatively just about sums up my teenage years. Do you like to hang out in your room alone and write, too? I think that makes us awesome!

~Brooke E. Wayne

memories are a prison
the next chapter in her life
detention is a dungeon
be an illuminated soul
in an ocean of happiness
mind set in stone
heart of gold
life is an open book
thirsty for victory
laugher is music to his ears
scream is a hammer to the head
hope is a garden, flourishing with care
you are my sunshine
an encyclopedia between his ears

_____

_____

_____

_____

_____

_____

_____

_____

Sometimes a metaphor is implied, meaning the item is
assumed to be something other than itself without being
stated as such directly. The 'is' or 'was' dissapears when
the metaphor is implied.

_____

_____

_____

_____

_____

_____

_____

_____

_____

_____

_____

_____

_____

_____

_____

_____

_____

_____

_____

_____

_____

_____

_____

_____

_____

_____

_____

_____

_____

_____

_____

_____

_____

_____

_____

_____

_____

_____

_____

_____

_____

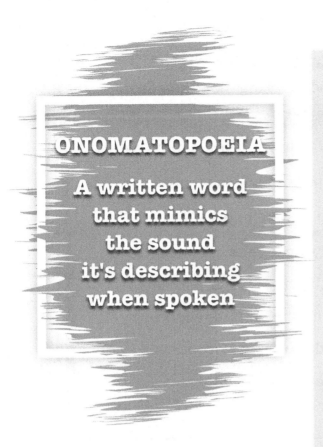

ONOMATOPOEIA

A written word that mimics the sound it's describing when spoken

"The Bells"

I.
"Hear the sledges with the bells—
Silver bells!
What a world of merriment their melody foretells!
How they tinkle, tinkle, tinkle,
In the icy air of night!"
(Excerpt)

by
Edgar Allan Poe

On the following page, you will see a brainstorming box with several prompts for you to use, tweak into something better, or ignore, if you want to. Fill the blank lines with your own ideas, too.

Dear Writer,
　You are probably all too familiar with the poetic device known as an onomatopoeia, even if you didn't know that's what it's called, or if you may never, ever be able to spell it correctly. That's all right. You know what it means, and you've probably practiced writing them a dozen times or more in elementary school.
　Onomatopoeias are words that make the sound they are describing when spoken outloud. They can seem childish--take boing or zoink for instance--but they can also be quite the enriching "trick" to add to a poem. This poetic device enhances the image a reader has in his or her mind about the poem through sound.
　Edgar Allan Poe's "The Bells" takes the reader through all the emotions, using countless sound effects. The poem reaches a haunting climax with the repetitive usage of some mind-boggling onomatopoeias. It's worth looking up the whole poem, but brace yourself, it's a doozy.
　Why don't you zip on over to the next page and start working on some one-liners to slip into a poem.

~Brooke E. Wayne

snap, kerplunk, swish, whoosh, zing, pow, splash, zip,
boing, hiss, whiz, splish, gulp, crunch, smack, zoink,
crackle, purr, gulp, zoom, growl, squish, snarl, moan, hum,
pop, splash, crisp, snap, plop, howl, crinkle, plop, whirl

snake <u>slithered</u> along the dusty trail

door <u>swung</u> open and <u>crashed</u> into the wall

stomach <u>gurgled</u> so loudly, everyone turned to look

water <u>trickled</u> over the riverbed of pebbles

siren <u>howled</u> alerting the neighborhood

abandoned house had <u>creaking</u> floorboards

porch swing <u>groaned</u> on its chains

_____

_____

_____

_____

_____

_____

_____

_____

_____

_____

_____

_____

Flip forward to page 51 for more sounds to use in your poetry.

_____

_____

_____

_____

_____

_____

_____

_____

_____

_____

_____

_____

_____

_____

_____

_____

_____

_____

_____

_____

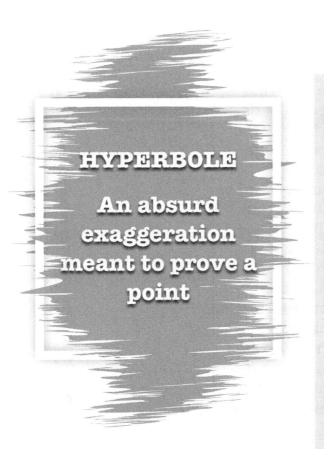

HYPERBOLE

An absurd exaggeration meant to prove a point

How Do I Love Thee?

"How do I love thee?
Let me count the ways.
I love thee
to the depth and breadth and height
my soul can reach,"
(Excerpt Sonnet 43)

by
Elizabeth Barrett Browning

On the following page, you will see a brainstorming box with several prompts for you to use, tweak into something better, or ignore, if you want to. Fill the blank lines with your own ideas, too.

Dear Writer,

When you blow something totally out of proportion through exaggeration, you're using the poetic device, hyperbole. It's pronounced "high-PER-bow-lee" incase you were still trying to figure that out in your head. You're welcome.

This little "trick" is a big way to create impact statements in your writing. It's one thing to say something is gianormous, but an entirely other to say it is so grand it deserves its own planet because the one we're parked on is too insufficient for its needs. Now that is a hyperbole.

In Browning's infamous poem about all the ways she is totally obsessing over some dude, she gets her point across through the use of several impossibly glorious exaggerations.

This device is fun to use and even overuse if you want because it has a unique way of making writing go from funny to hysterical. (See what I did there?)

Now, go write some absurdly grand poetry on the next few pages.

~Brooke E. Wayne

ride like the wind
floating on clouds
tear into the person
boiling with rage
cry a river
walk five hundred miles
try a thousand times
told a million ways
weighed a ton
sky scraper (tall building)
ocean of love
mountain of homework to climb
blindingly bright smile
piled high as the sky
shoes are killing me
died when I saw him
to the moon and back again

_____

_____

_____

_____

_____

_____

_____

_____

_____

Example: My buddy's joke was so old it was as hunched over and gasping for air as I was having to listen to it for the billionth time. He needs to step up his game for attention.

_____

_____

_____

_____

_____

_____

_____

_____

_____

_____

_____

_____

_____

_____

_____

_____

_____

_____

_____

_____

_____

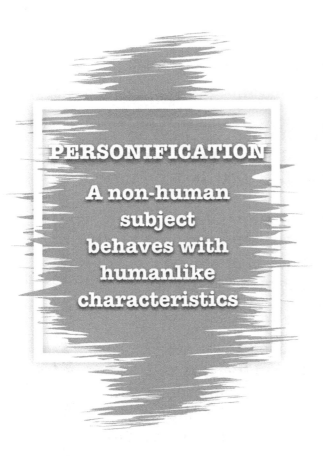

PERSONIFICATION

A non-human subject behaves with humanlike characteristics

I Wandered Lonely as a Cloud

"I wandered lonely as a Cloud
That floats on high o'er Vales and Hills,
When all at once I saw a crowd,
A host of golden Daffodils;
Beside the Lake, beneath the trees,
Fluttering and dancing in the breeze."
(Excerpt)

by
William Wordsworth

On the following page, you will see a brainstorming box with several prompts for you to use, tweak into something better, or ignore, if you want to. Fill the blank lines with your own ideas, too.

Dear Writer,

In William Wordsworth's poem, he lounges on his couch with his eyes squeezed closed remembering when he had seen a field of thousands of daffoldils in all their glory. Daffodils are those yellow or white flowers that look like teacups. They bloom during springtime, and with their long slender stems, they tend to sway and dip as if in celebration when the least bit of breeze tousles their spritely blooms. Wordsworth uses the poetic device of personification to capture a field of daffodils having a secret party beside a lake and beneath some trees.

Since flowers, though alive, are not of the human species, they cannot dance, but when the "trick" of personification is applied to their actions, they most certainly can. Adding this device to objects in a poem gives the reader something more to imagine as inanimate items start to come alive.

What lifeless thing do you want to breathe physical attributes into in your poetry? I'm sure whatever you choose, you'll captivate the imagination of your readers!

~Brooke E. Wayne

ACTION WORDS:

ran, skipped, chuckled, sang, tricked, laughed, taunted, screeched, howled, wished, dreamt, held, bartered, spoke, basked, danced, raged, tickled, lied, promised

... breeze caressing my face
... leaves dancing on the tree
... hope clinging to her every word
... alarm screaming at me to wake up
... boredom stealing my mood

The video game enchanted the players.
The song curled around her heart.
The soccer ball cried for help during the game.
The test mocked me with its difficulty.
The blank sheet of paper whispered, "I'm waiting."

Sports cars have attitude.
Netflix keeps calling to me.
Comfort wraps its arms around me.
Words creep onto my page.
Books give me nothing but love.

_____
_____
_____
_____
_____
_____
_____
_____

_____

_____

_____

_____

_____

_____

_____

_____

_____

_____

_____

_____

_____

_____

_____

_____

_____

_____

_____

_____

_____

_____

_____

_____

_____

_____

_____

_____

_____

_____

_____

_____

_____

_____

_____

_____

_____

_____

REPETITION

Repeating a word, phrase, line, stanza, concept, or rhythmical pattern in a poem

Properly Scholarly Attitude

"The poet pursues his beautiful theme;
The preacher his golden beatitude;
And I run after a vanishing dream–
The glittering, will-o'-the-wispish gleam
Of the properly scholarly attitude–
The highly desirable, the very
advisable,
The hardly acquirable, properly
scholarly attitude."
(Excerpt)

by
Adelaide Crapsey

On the following page, you will see a brainstorming box with several prompts for you to use, tweak into something better, or ignore, if you want to. Fill the blank lines with your own ideas, too.

Dear Writer,

It doesn't get any easier than the "trick" of repeating something in a poem. That's literally all there is to it. What you choose to put on a loop is up to you.

You can use the poetic device of repetition to say the same word or similar words over and over--think synonyms--or even repeat a phrase, line, or a whole stanze if you want to.

Look at Crapsey's example and see how she repeats specific words that also happen to be the title of the poem. This device causes the reader to remember specific messages in a poem. It also causes the reader to develop a specific feeling about the poem, too.

Repetition is not only confined to words, but it can also be the repeating of rhythmical patterns as felt in the example, as well.

Write out an impact statement (or phrase) and wrap a bunch of other creative words around it, then put repetition to use with that statement or phrase, and watch your poem go from interesting to spectacular.

~Brooke E. Wayne

Repetition of Similar Words:

beautiful, pretty, lovely, attractive
gross, disgusting, revolting, awful
happy, joyful, jubilant, pleased
angry, disgruntled, mad, upset

Repetition of Phrases:

then the sun rose
for the love of liberty
while I walked away
because I knew she would
when the darkness fell
stood still as stone

Repetition of Lines:

I had reached the end of it.
They walked together, two by two.
Only the truth could be told.
It took my breath away.
Freedom found a way today.

_____
_____
_____
_____
_____
_____
_____
_____
_____

_____

_____

_____

_____

_____

_____

_____

_____

_____

_____

_____

_____

_____

_____

_____

_____

_____

_____

_____

_____

_____

_____

_____

_____

_____

_____

_____

_____

_____

_____

_____

_____

_____

_____

_____

_____

_____

_____

_____

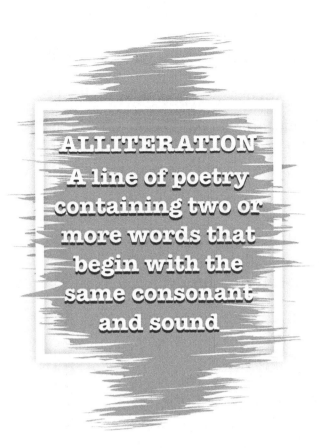

ALLITERATION
A line of poetry containing two or more words that begin with the same consonant and sound

The Eagle

"He clasps the crag with crooked hands;
Close to the sun in lonely lands,
Ringed with the azure world, he stands."
(Excerpt)

by
Alfred Lord Tennyson

On the following page, you will see a brainstorming box with several prompts for you to use, tweak into something better, or ignore, if you want to. Fill the blank lines with your own ideas, too.

Dear Writer,

Most people automatically think of tongue twisters when they think of Alliteration, and rightfully so. Those little spoken puzzles are all about using this "trick". All you have to do is pack in two or more words with the same consonant sound into a line of poetry, and there you go--you have the beginnings of a tantalizing tongue twister.

Just so you know though, no one is going to judge you if you want to make some alliterative phrases out of vowel sounds, too.

Alliteration is a fantastic poetic device for making poetry really feel and sound like poetry, whether the words are read silently in someone's noggin or spoken out loud. Alliteration creates a sing-songy lilt to creative writing. It's almost like a topsy-turvy kind of dance, if you will.

You might have noticed alliteration being used all the time to create catchy titles for activities, clubs, slogans, and world-wide events. For example, "Taco Tuesday!" or "Dunkin' Donuts", even "Paypal" makes use of this poetic device.

Pack some of your poetic lines with this mellifluous device, and listen to the way your writing goes from meh to magnificent.
Brooke E. Wayne

Alliteration as Tongue Twisters:

Rachel read a really ridiculous riddle.
Merry memories made for a magical moment.
Nobody needs notes, not now not ever.

Alliteration Clusters:

wild wind whipped whimsically
bright bubbly beautiful babies
haunting howling horrifying house

Alliteration Pairs:

crisp cold
sharp shards
salty seafoam
dry desert
brilliant besties
heavenly happiness
tracing time
friends forever
lilting laughter

_____

_____

_____

_____

_____

_____

_____

_____

_____

_____

_____

_____

_____

_____

_____

_____

_____

_____

_____

_____

_____

_____

_____

_____

_____

_____

_____

_____

_____

_____

_____

_____

_____

_____

_____

_____

_____

_____

_____

_____

_____

_____

_____

_____

_____

_____

_____

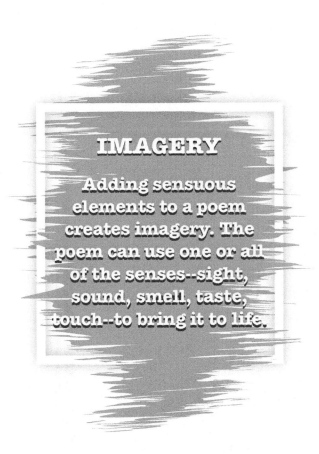

IMAGERY

Adding sensuous elements to a poem creates imagery. The poem can use one or all of the senses--sight, sound, smell, taste, touch--to bring it to life.

To the Thawing Wind

"Come with rain, O loud Southwester!
Bring the singer, bring the nester;
Give the buried flower a dream;
Make the settled snowbank steam;"
(Excerpt)

by
Robert Frost

On the following page, you will see a brainstorming box with several prompts for you to use, tweak into something better, or ignore, if you want to. Fill the blank lines with your own ideas, too.

Dear Writer,

Notice how Robert Frost's poem is so visually popping! Mentally listen to the way he brings to life the sound of rainfall and the howling wind in this snipet from his famous poem. Imagery is the "trick" that creates vivid, stimulating experiences for our readers.

This poetic device has five parts to it. Imagery makes use of any of the senses--sight, sound, smell, taste, and touch. In case you didn't realize it, colors count, too. Colorful words ignite the sight imagery just as well as describing a specific object does. You don't have to put every single one of the senses into a poem, though, for this poetic device to be considered in use. Only add the sensuous element if it enhances the poem you are writing, not clutters it.

Sensuous words tap into the reader's imagination, providing them with a mental movie to romp around in, so use this device precisely to express what you want your reader to experience.

~Brooke E. Wayne

Imagery:
Sight, Sound, Smell, Taste, Touch

I have created several sensuous lists
on pages 46-49
that cover all the senses of Imagery,
as well as basic colors
and all their various hues,
which count for sight.
Use words from these lists
to add to your creative writing.
Below, you will see some
prompt phrases and one-liners
that incorporate sensory elements.

Phrases & One-Liners

a misty rain whispers secrets
shimmering waves call to me
bright, flickering lights
pungeant earth after a downpour
sticky sweet billows of cotton candy
sparkling effervescence over ice

_____

_____

_____

_____

_____

_____

_____

_____

_____

_____

_____

_____

_____

_____

_____

_____

_____

_____

_____

_____

_____

_____

_____

_____

_____

The
Sensuous
World

Hey? Psst! Once upon a time, when I was a middle
schooler, I became obsessed with a novel called
The Outsiders, by S. E. Hinton, which, if you haven't
already had to read this book, is the ultimate
coming-of-age story for teenagers worldwide.
What impacted me most about this novel
is how important it is to pause life
and watch the sunset--or sunrise--because
it can do wonders for the soul.
I would wake up early every day before school
and watch ribbons of peach and powder pink
wind their way through the sapphire sky,
as the sun edged away the darkness of morning
from my kitchen table.
Sometimes, I would even park on a hill overlooking
the valley I lived in and sit on the hood of my car,
watching that same sun slowly slip away,
leaving tangerine and fuchsia in its wake
like paint swipes on a tree-lined canvas.
What did I get out of sun-watching?
Serenity. Mindfulness. Hope. Closer to God.
Closer to me. Flash forward, and I've spent the last 25
years teaching The Outsiders
and encouraging teenagers to stay gold,
and seek out a little pause in life with the sun.
If you haven't done this yet, try it.
Even if you think you're alone, I can assure you,
thousands are watching that sun with you, too,
figuring out their own journey, just like you.

IMAGERY

SIGHT	SOUND	TASTE	TOUCH	SCENT
All Colors	Onomatopoeias	Acidic	Abrasive	Aromatic
All Sizes	Barking	Acrid	Bristly	Briny
Bold	Breathy	Bitter	Bumpy	Burnt
Bright	Buzzing	Bittersweet	Clammy	Citrusy
Brilliant	Clanking	Bland	Cold	Dank
Cluttered	Clomping	Buttery	Creamy	Dusty
Curled	Croaky	Chalky	Doughy	Earthy
Curved	Crispy	Chocolaty	Fluffy	Fishy
Dark	Crunchy	Fresh	Furry	Floral
Dim	Dripping	Fruity	Humid	Foul
Dingy	Gong	Honeyed	Greasy	Fragrant
Dull	Groan	Lemony	Grimy	Full-bodied
Faded	Gurgle	Metallic	Gritty	Gamy
Foggy	Gutteral	Minty	Hairy	Garlicky
Glittery	Hoarse	Nutty	Hot	Herbal
Gloomy	Hiss	Raw	Icy	Malted
Glossy	Huff	Resfreshing	Jellied	Metallic
Hazy	Husky	Rich	Leathery	Moldy
Illuminating	Moan	Ripe	Liquid	Musty
Illustrious	Murmur	Roasted	Mushy	Peppery
Iridescent	Peep	Robust	Oily	Perfumed
Milky	Purring	Rotten	Powdery	Piney
Misty	Ringing	Salty	Prickly	Pungent
Murky	Rustle	Savory	Rough	Putrid
Pale	Shrilling	Smoked	Sandy	Rancid
Shabby	Sizzle	Soupy	Satiny	Rank
Shimmering	Slur	Sour	Scalding	Rotten
Shiny	Snivel	Spicy	Silky	Salty
Smudged	Strangled	Stale	Slick	Seasoned
Sparkling	Swoosh	Succulent	Soft	Smoky
Spotted	Thud	Sugary	Stiff	Spiced
Spreckled	Thumping	Sweet	Smooth	Spoiled
Straight	Tinkling	Syrupy	Sticky	Sulfuric
Wizened	Trickling	Tangy	Sultry	Stinky
Worn	Whisper	Tart	Velvety	Woodsy

REDS	ORANGES	YELLOWS	GREENS
Amaranth	Amber	Almond	Algae
Baby Pink	Apricot	Banana	Apple
Beet	Auburn	Biscotti	Army
Berry	Begonia	Bisque	Avocado
Blood	Bird of Paradise	Blond	Basil
Blush	Bronze	Brass	Celadon
Bordeaux	Burnt	Buff	Celery
Brick	Cantaloupe	Buttercup	Chartreuse
Bubblegum	Carrot	Buttermilk	Chayote
Burgundy	Cheddar	Butternut	Citron
Cabernet	Chrysanthemum	Butterscotch	Clover
Candy Apple	Cider	Camel	Crocodile
Cardinal	Cinnabar	Canary	Emerald
Carnation	Clementine	Candlelight	Evergreen
Cayenne	Copper	Champagne	Forest
Cerise	Coral	Cheesecake	Grass
Cherry	Creamsicle	Citrine	Grasshopper
Chili	Fire	Corn	Honeydew
Cinnamon	Flame	Cream	Hunter
Claret	Fox	Curry	Jade
Cotton Candy	Ginger	Custard	Juniper
Cranberry	Lava	Daffodil	Kelly
Crimson	Mandarin	Daisy	Khaki
Currant	Mango	Dandelion	Kiwi
Dragonfruit	Marigold	Dijon	Laurel
Fire Engine	Marmalade	Ecru	Leaf
Flamingo	Melon	Flaxen	Lettuce
Garnet	Navel	Gold	Lime
Hot Pink	Papaya	Goldenrod	Margarita
Lipstick	Peach	Harvest	Mint
Magenta	Persimmon	Honey	Mistletoe
Maroon	Poppy	Honeysuckle	Moss
Mauve	Pumpkin	Lemon	Olive
Paprika	Russet	Mustard	Pea
Pomegranate	Rust	Nude	Pea Soup
Punch	Saffron	Oatmeal	Peridot
Raspberry	Salamander	Ochre	Pickle
Rose	Salmon	Pear	Pine
Rouge	Sherbet	Pearl	Pistachio
Ruby	Sienna	Pineapple	Sage
Ruddy	Spice	Sand	Sea Glass
Sangria	Squash	Shortbread	Seaweed
Scarlet	Sulfur	Sunflower	Spring
Strawberry	Sunset	Straw	Spruce
Tea Rose	Tangerine	Tan	Green Tea
Tomato	Terra Cotta	Tawny	Teal
Watermelon	Tiger	Topaz	Tourmaline
Vermilion	Titian	Tuscany	Willow
Vixen	Yam	Vintage	Wintergreen

BLUES	PURPLES	BROWNS	YOUR LIST
Admiral	Amethyst	Beige	_____
Aegean	Blackberry	Birch	_____
Aqua	Boysenberry	Brunette	_____
Aquamarine	Byzantine	Cappuccino	_____
Azure	Concord	Caramel	_____
Baby Blue	Eggplant	Cedar	_____
Blue Bell	Grape	Chestnut	_____
Blueberry	Heather	Chocolate	_____
British	Hibiscus	Coffee	_____
Cadet	Hydrangea	Fawn	_____
Capri	Lavender	Hazelnut	_____
Caribbean	Lilac	Hickory	_____
Celestial	Merlot	Leather	_____
Cerulean	Mulberry	Mahogany	_____
Cobalt	Orchid	Mocha	_____
Cornflower	Periwinkle	Nutmeg	_____
Cyan	Plum	Oak	_____
Delphinium	Violet	Pecan	_____
Denim	Wisteria	Russet	_____
Egyptian		Sand	_____
Electric	**WHITES**	Sandalwood	_____
Forget-Me-Not		Sandstone	_____
Geranium		Sepia	_____
Hyacinth	Alabaster	Tan	_____
Imperial	Antique	Toffee	_____
Indigo	Ash	Redwood	_____
Iris	Bone	Rust	_____
Lagoon	Cloud	Walnut	_____
Lake	Crystal	Wheat	_____
Lapis	Diamond		_____
Larimar	Dove	**BLACKS**	_____
Midnight	Eggshell		_____
Navy	Frost		_____
Ocean	Ice	Charcoal	_____
Oxford	Ivory	Ebony	_____
Peacock	Lace	Granite	_____
Persian	Marble	Graphite	_____
Powder	Marshmallow	Gray	_____
Robin's Egg	Mist	Gun Metal	_____
Royal	Opal	Ink	_____
Sapphire	Oyster	Jet	_____
Sea Foam	Paper	Obsidian	_____
Sky	Parchment	Onyx	_____
Slate blue	Pearl	Pewter	_____
Teal	Platinum	Pitch	_____
Tiffany	Porcelain	Sable	_____
Topaz	Silver	Smoke	_____
Tropical	Snow	Soot	_____
Turquoise	Sugar	Steel	_____
Ultramarine	Vanilla	Stone	_____

PERSONALITY TRAITS & EMOTIONS

Adventurous	Fake	Knowledgeable	Popular	————
Affectionate	Fancy	Kooky	Quaint	————
Aggressive	Foolish	Laughable	Quick	————
Altruistic	Forgetful	Lazy	Quiet	————
Ambitious	Fortunate	Liberal	Quizzical	————
Appropriate	Friendly	Logical	Radical	————
Artistic	Funny	Lonely	Ravishing	————
Blessed	Gallant	Loquacious	Realistic	————
Boisterous	Gentle	Loud	Reclusive	————
Boring	Giddy	Maddening	Reserved	————
Brave	Gracious	Magical	Sad	————
Brilliant	Guilty	Mature	Sappy	————
Bubbly	Gullible	Merry	Sarcastic	————
Caring	Happy	Mischievous	Serene	————
Clever	Hasty	Mystical	Shy	————
Comical	Hateful	Natural	Smart	————
Courageous	Helpful	Naughty	Sophisticated	————
Cowardly	Hesitant	Nefarious	Studious	————
Crafty	Honest	Nervous	Subdued	————
Creative	Humble	Nice	Talented	————
Defensive	Hyperactive	Noble	Tenderhearted	————
Depressed	Idealistic	Nonsensical	Thoughtful	————
Discordant	Imaginative	Oblivious	Tormented	————
Dreamy	Immature	Obnoxious	Tricky	————
Dull	Innovative	Obsessive	Underrated	————
Elated	Intelligent	Opinionated	Uppity	————
Energetic	Introverted	Optimistic	Upset	————
Ethical	Jealous	Outgoing	Visionary	————
Excited	Jovial	Outlandish	Whimsical	————
Expectant	Joyful	Outspoken	Wild	————
Extravagant	Jubilant	Passive	Wise	————
Extroverted	Keen	Pessimistic	Wistful	————
Fabulous	Kind	Pleasing	Youthful	————

COLOR ME

DIRECTIONS: On the following page, you will see the same poem as this one with all the fill-in-the-blank spaces awaiting your personal touch. Look through the Imagery, Color, and Personality Traits/Emotions Lists to find words that are meaningful to you. Then create your own Color Me poem. Once you complete the template, rewrite it again neatly on the journal page.

COLOR ME PINK

Color me pink--
The color of tenderness.
Don't shade me in a boisterous, hyperactive, laughable yellow.
That's not who I am.
Color me bubblegum, flamingo, lipstick pink.
It's so much more my style.
I'm not a fake, boring, orange,
Or a gullible, cowardly, blue.
Just a jovial, creative, elegant pink.
That's the color I'll be.
I'm the color of fragrant flower petals
On a cool, spring day,
The color of a quiet corner in a busy room
Where I can write my poetry.
Color me gracious,
Color me serene.
I'm pink. That's what I am.
That's the color of me.

by
Brooke E. Wayne

COLOR ME _____
basic color

Color me _____
basic color

The color of _____.
abstract noun

Don't shade me in a _____, _____, _____ _____.
three unlike personality traits or emotions   unlike color

That's not who I am.

Color me _____, _____, _____ _____.
three different shades of the basic color   basic color

It's so much more my style.

I'm not a/an _____, _____, _____,
two unlike personality traits or emotions   unlike color

Or a/an _____, _____, _____.
two unlike personality traits or emotions   unlike color

Just a/an _____, _____, _____ _____.
three personality traits or emotions   basic color

That's the color I'll be.

I'm the color of _____
describe an object or a scene metaphorically

_____,

The color of a/an _____
describe an object or a scene metaphorically

_____.

Color me _____,
emotion

Color me _____.
emotion

I'm _____. **That's what I am.**
basic color

That's the color of me.

by

_____

_____

_____

_____

_____

_____

_____

_____

_____

_____

_____

_____

_____

_____

_____

_____

_____

_____

_____

_____

_____

_____

_____

_____

A DAY AT THE BEACH

DIRECTIONS: On the following pages, you will see a list of questions to guide you in writing your own sensuous poem that utilizes imagery--sight, sound, smell, taste, and touch. You can see several additional poetic devices in this example poem, as well, such as alliteration, personification, and implied metaphors. Be sure to add several words from the Imagery, Color, and Personality Traits/Emotions Lists to enhance your poetry's senses.

A Day at the Beach

Sticky ice cream
drools down the knuckles
of a freckle-faced boy,
sun-kissed
with the beginnings
of treasured memories.
A salty, summer breeze,
thick with children's laughter,
captures their boisterous joy,
as thunderous waves
topple towards
the sugar-white shore,
clamoring for their feet.
Seagulls chatter in response,
drifting carefree
against the mirrored,
ice-blue sky.

by
Brooke E. Wayne

BRAINSTORM

Pick a location: (beach, mountains, city, etc.)

What do you see?

What do you smell?

What sounds do you hear?

What do you taste?

What textures do you touch?

How does this location make you feel? (List emotions in the form of nouns. For example: 'happy' becomes 'happiness')

Create Similes (or Metaphors) with these emotions:

My (noun) is like a/an (object) that (action with imagery words).

Example: My happiness is like a dolphin that bursts through the waves, spinning around before plunging beneath the turquoise water again.

Create Personification with an object: (Example: sand 'tickles" toes)

_____

_____

_____

_____

_____

_____

_____

_____

_____

_____

_____

_____

_____

_____

_____

_____

_____

_____

_____

_____

_____

_____

_____

_____

_____

_____

_____

_____

_____

_____

_____

_____

_____

_____

_____

_____

_____

_____

_____

_____

_____

_____

_____

_____

BORING
TO BRILLIANT

DIRECTIONS: You will turn a boring starter prompt into a brilliant poem.

Do you notice how the boring poem starter below has five syllables per line and reads with a monotonous cadence?

You will write poetry based on a few prompts, turning the boring starters into works of literary art that have varying sentence structures and lengths. By doing this, it creates a musical effect when a poem is being read.

I created a Brilliant Revamp of the first Boring Starter Prompt for you on the next page for you to study. Compare the two writings, and see if you can identify all the poetic devices and words from the lists that I used to write the new and improved poem. Then begin your own Brilliant Poetry using the other prompt starters.

Be sure to include as many details from the Imagery, Colors, and Personality Traits/Emotions Lists as you want to improve your poetry.

BORING STARTER PROMPT:

A man rode a horse.
He went through the woods.
The sun was so hot.
Birds circled above.
The ground was dusty.

BORING TO BRILLIANT

The Great Escape

Naked branches tore at the man's shirt,
gnarled and twisted,
bending their claws in desperation,
as he broke free from the parched woods.
They were closing in.
A merciless heat beat down on the wasteland.
Desolate.
Wrought with lifeless wreckage
caused by the blistering sun.
His wild horse,
never faltering once,
pressed forward upon the scorched riverbed.
Hot breath burst from the beast's flaring nostrils.
Closer still.
Men's cries rang out.
Their gunshots shattered dark birds against the stark white sky,
once drifting in aimless circles.
His freedom neared.
He could see it just over the horizon.
Sensing the man's adrenaline, his horse bore down,
and dust hung suspended in the wake of their escape.

by
Brooke E. Wayne

BORING TO BRILLIANT

BORING STARTER PROMPT

The teen(s) saw the house.
It was abandoned.
He/she/they walked up the steps.
The door swung open.
He/she/they walked through the door.
He/she/they looked all around.

_____

_____

_____

_____

_____

_____

_____

_____

_____

_____

_____

_____

_____

_____

_____

by

_____

BORING
TO BRILLIANT

BORING STARTER PROMPT

I walked into the room.
Everyone turned towards me.
I began to speak out.
I spoke to them with hope.
They all listened to me.

_____

_____

_____

_____

_____

_____

_____

_____

_____

_____

_____

_____

_____

_____

_____

by

_____

BORING TO BRILLIANT

BORING STARTER PROMPT

The rain fell upon my head.
I saw things in the distance.
I took slow steps towards the edge.
No one knew I was coming.
I didn't even feel cold.

_____

_____

_____

_____

_____

_____

_____

_____

_____

_____

_____

_____

_____

_____

by

_____

BORING TO BRILLIANT

BORING STARTER PROMPT

My heart was full of peace.
I had everything now.
My life felt so complete.
No one could stop me now.
I made it to the top.

_____

_____

_____

_____

_____

_____

_____

_____

_____

_____

_____

_____

_____

_____

by

_____

WRITE

_____

_____

_____

_____

_____

_____

_____

_____

_____

_____

_____

_____

_____

_____

_____

_____

_____

_____

_____

_____

Prompts

Hey? Psst! Some people can sit down
with a blank piece of paper
and words will magically appear
in their thought bubble
floating above their heads
for them to fill the paper with,
and that's okay.
Others need a little help getting started.
This next section
contains lots of vocabulary terms
and a variety of prompts
for you to fill
your own thought bubble with.
You can change the prompts
any way you want to.
Each poetic starter is meant to inspire
not confine your creativity.
Be sure to grab a handful
of wondrous words
along with some poetic devices
to sprinkle into your poems.
You can even do some pre-writing
in the brainstorming boxes provided, too,
if that's more your style.
Either way, I'll be over here cheering you on!

PROMPT # 1

You get up, you get ready, you go to school, and then what?
Take your reader on a journey through a
DAY IN THE LIFE OF YOUR SHOES.

STYLE: Free Verse, Narrative
(Narratives have a beginning, middle, and end, telling a complete story)

TWIST: Alternate Objects
Hat, Jersey, Team Shirt, Necklace, Ring, Bracelet, Bike, Scooter, Journal

POINT-OF-VIEW: 1st Person from the perspective of your shoes (or other object)

PROMPT # 2

The emotion of <u>hope</u> is often written of an <u>anchor</u>,
tethering one's feelings with certainty to a brighter future.

Choose another **EMOTION** and transform it into an object,
using a **METAPHOR** as the poetic device to bring your emotion substance.

EXAMPLES:
ANGER–Freight Train, LOVE–Blooming Flower, PEACE–Warm Blanket

STYLE:
Rhyme Scheme: abcb, defe, ghih

_____

_____

_____

_____

_____

_____

_____

_____

_____

_____

_____

_____

_____

_____

_____

_____

_____

_____

_____

_____

_____

_____

_____

_____

_____

_____

_____

_____

_____

_____

_____

_____

_____

_____

_____

_____

_____

_____

_____

_____

_____

_____

_____

_____

_____

_____

_____

_____

_____

_____

_____

_____

_____

_____

_____

_____

_____

_____

_____

_____

WONDROUS WORDS

AMPLE: (adj) Sufficient in amount
We had ample time to complete the task.

CORDIAL: (adj) Friendly, polite
The host of the party was cordial to all her guests.

FUTILE: (adj) Having no purpose or effect
It was futile for us to keep trying to get the machine to work.

LINGER: (v) To remain in a place longer than necessary
She lingered behind her friends, gazing at the painting a little longer.

PROMINENT: (adj) Standing out, noticeable
Her bright green eyes were her most prominent feature.

QUENCH: (v) To satisfy one's thirst
He wanted to quench his thirst with an ice-cold sports drink.

ROBUST: (adj) Strong or flavorful
The robust taste of the coffee made her scrunch up her nose.

UNIQUE: (adj) Distinct or uncommon
The artwork was so unique they gazed at it for several minutes, studying its beauty.

UTMOST: (adj) Greatest or most extreme
It was the utmost competition with a prize of a million dollars.

WHIM: (noun) Impulse, a sudden change of mind
She shifted her plans to travel on a whim and ended up going to another country.

CREATIVE WRITING STARTER:

I quenched my thirst for adventure, abandoning my futile habits along the way,
No longer lingering on doubts, while my whimsical, new hopes took flight ...

PROMPT # 3

Make a list of all the things in your life that bring you COMFORT.
Turn each item on your list into a SIMILE.
Create a FREE VERSE poem of one-liners celebrating what comforts you.

EXAMPLES:
Comfort is like a warm meal ...
Comfort is like a cozy pair of sweats ...
Comfort is like the sound of my baby sister's laughter ...

TWIST:
Use a different emotion for every line in your poem.

PROMPT # 4

Write a <u>Rhyming Poem</u> loaded with <u>Alliteration</u>
and centered around your personal
MANTRA
A Mantra is like a saying, caption, motto, or philosophy you live by.

EXAMPLES:
Stay Sweet–Strive Strong
To Give Up or Give In is to Quit
To Move On or Move Over is to Start Anew
Everyday is a New Path of Possibilities

_____

_____

_____

_____

_____

_____

_____

_____

_____

_____

_____

_____

_____

_____

_____

_____

_____

_____

_____

WONDROUS WORDS

ASPIRE: (v) Focus one's hopes towards achieving something
He aspires to be a professional athlete.

AWE: (n) A sensation of fear with reverence and wonder
She was in awe as she watched the fireworks explode directly above her.

ELUDE: (v) To avoid or escape from danger
In order to elude the falling rocks, they took a different route.

ENCOUNTER: (v) To have an unpleasant chance meeting
Their encounter with the cougar along the trail terrified them.

IMMENSE: (adj) Extremely large in size, amount, or degree
An immense amount of driftwood washed up on the shore after the storm.

JOVIAL: (adj) Jolly or cheerful
Her jovial personality drew others to her.

LOLL: (v) To lounge or sprawl out in a lazy way
He was lolling about all afternoon, watching TV and playing video games.

PONDER: (v) To wonder about something thoughtfully
She pondered over whether she should attend the event or not.

TARRY: (v) To wait, delay, or be tardy
If they tarry any longer in the park, they'll miss their train home.

VIE: (v) To compete for superiority
They both challenged each other in order to vie for the grand prize.

CREATIVE WRITING STARTER:

Inspiration cannot elude me any longer as I tarry in the garden,
surrounded by jovial blooms welcoming spring with immense bursts of color ...

PROMPT # 5

Have you ever received excellent **ADVICE** from someone
or given advice that truly helped the person you shared it with?
What was it? Can you translate it into a poem?

STYLE:
1st Person Point-of-View
RHYME SCHEMES:
abab cdcd efef ghgh, abba cddc effe ghhg
POETIC DEVICES:
Metaphor–Turn emotions into objects
Personification–Give words physical attributes

PROMPT # 6

One day, you slam your fist against the bank of lockers,
and one of them on the end that has always been jammed pops open unexpectedly.
You peer inside and discover a **HIDDEN WORLD** lurks behind its dented façade.
Do you climb through alone or go grab some friends to discover what lurks ahead?

Write a Narrative Poem that stars you (and your friends)
and what happens when you crawl through the portal and start prowling around.

POETIC DEVICES:
Imagery, Personification, Repetition

_____

_____

_____

_____

_____

_____

_____

_____

_____

_____

_____

_____

_____

_____

_____

_____

_____

_____

_____

_____

_____

_____

_____

_____

_____

_____

_____

_____

_____

_____

_____

_____

_____

_____

_____

_____

_____

_____

_____

_____

_____

_____

_____

_____

_____

_____

_____

_____

_____

_____

_____

_____

_____

_____

_____

_____

_____

_____

_____

_____

_____

_____

WONDROUS WORDS

ABANDON: (v) To leave behind
She had to <u>abandon</u> the idea because there was no way it could work.

BLUNDER: (v) To make a foolish mistake
The <u>blunder</u> he made on the project caused him to start it over completely.

DEPLETE: (v) To empty or consume until gone
With depleted food supplies, they had to cut their camping trip short.

FRUITLESS: (adj) Unproductive, unable to accomplish desired effect
Her efforts were <u>fruitless</u>, so she gave up.

GRUELING: (adj) Extremely exhausting or demanding
The game was so grueling on the players but worth it when they won.

INSTILL: (v) Gradually put an idea in someone's mind
The teacher wanted to <u>instill</u> in her students a sense of self-worth.

MUSE: (v) To be consumed by thoughts
She mused about the possibility of accomplishing her goals for the day.

TREACHEROUS: (adj) Unreliable, likely to betray trust
The bridge proved to be <u>treacherous</u> when the boards began to crack.

ULTIMATE: (adj) The final stage of a process
The <u>ultimate</u> challenge took hours before he finally beat the game.

WRANGLED: (v) to argue or bicker
He <u>wrangled</u> with his little brother over who had to do the chores.

CREATIVE WRITING STARTER:

I abandoned my fears and became <u>instilled</u> with the belief that I could reach my goals,
and, though the challenges I faced would be <u>treacherous</u>, I knew I would succeed ...

PROMPT # 7

Starting out is the hardest part of writing for some people.
Below are several **HALF ONE-LINERS** to jumpstart your poem.
Write a free-verse or rhyming poem, and load it with as many poetic devices as you want.
You can even write several poems if you feel inspired by more than one poem starter!

OPENING LINES:
I woke up to the roaring sound of ...
Mirror, you amaze me, pulling me into your ...
Three ways you've made me happy, three times you've made me laugh ...
If I could talk to ... the things that I would say ...
When I think about my future, I wonder ...

PROMPT # 8

GROWING UP is inevitable. We can't stop it. We can't skip over it.
We can control how we handle it, though.
For this poem, think about all the challenges you are facing right now,
and think of ways you can approach them, like holding your head high, chin-up,
one step at a time, one day at a time, with strength or with care,
diving head-first into those growing pains with a warrior's attitude,
or rising above the stress, like an eagle soaring above the storm.

Use one of the phrases above to create a poem about your experiences
as you are abandoning your childish ways and entering that stage in your life
where you begin to figure out who you are and what you're about.

_____

_____

_____

_____

_____

_____

_____

_____

_____

_____

_____

_____

_____

_____

_____

_____

_____

_____

_____

_____

_____

_____

_____

_____

_____

_____

_____

_____

_____

_____

_____

_____

_____

_____

_____

_____

_____

_____

_____

_____

WONDROUS WORDS

APPREHENSIVE: (adj) Worried something bad will happen
She was apprehensive about taking the test because she didn't study.

EERIE: (adj) Terrifying or peculiar
The abandoned house had an eerie feel to it with cobwebs everywhere.

HOAX: (noun) A comical or evil deception
The hoax they played on their friends left all of them screaming and laughing together.

MERE: (adj) Only what is made clear, no more or less
Only a mere amount of repair had been done, but it functioned.

OMNISCIENT: (adj) Being all-knowing
The book had an omniscient narrator who described everyone's thoughts.

PLUMMET: (v) To plunge or fall with great speed
The roller coaster plummeted from a peak of eighty feet, straight down.

SULKY: (adj) Moody, gloomy
His sulky attitude worried all of his friends because he was usually upbeat.

TEEMING: (adj) Crowded or full
The room was teeming with so many people, they had to split up to get through the crowd.

VORACIOUS: (adj) Wanting or eating large amounts of food
His voracious appetite led him to eat a whole loaf of bread with butter and jam.

UNRULY: (adj) Unable to be controlled, disorderly
The unruly crowd caused the concert to end sooner than planned for safety reasons.

CREATIVE WRITING STARTER:

No longer was I apprehensive to plummet into pursuing my hopes and dreams.
My mind teemed with plans, and my voracious appetite for success drove me ...

PROMPT # 9

What if you were in charge of all the RULES?
What would you make everyone abide by at home? At school? On weekends?
Would there be chaos or so much order, everyone would live like ants in a colony?
Would you be the center of everything, or would you tuck yourself in a corner and observe?

STYLE:
Write a Lyric Poem, giving a small glimpse of a scene
where everyone is following your rules.
(Lyric Poetry Lesson is on p. 143.)
Describe what the scene looks like using IMAGERY.
Add some REPETITION.
You could use the One-Liner: When I ruled the world!

PROMPT # 10

If friendship was a RECIPE, what ingredients would you put in it to create the perfect friend?

STYLE:
Free Verse
Write the poem like you would a regular recipe with an ingredients list.
Then describe the order and amounts of each ingredient
and how long it needs to bake to perfection.

POETIC DEVICES:
Turn each ingredient into a characteristic or attribute like loyal, kind, dependable
and create a METAPHOR or SIMILE for each of them in your description.

WRITE

_____

_____

_____

_____

_____

_____

_____

_____

_____

_____

_____

_____

_____

_____

_____

_____

_____

_____

_____

_____

_____

_____

_____

_____

_____

_____

_____

_____

_____

_____

_____

_____

_____

_____

_____

_____

_____

_____

_____

_____

_____

_____

_____

_____

_____

_____

_____

_____

_____

_____

_____

_____

_____

_____

_____

_____

_____

_____

_____

_____

WONDROUS WORDS

ABUNDANT: (adj) Plentiful
She had an abundant amount of gum, so she shared the pack with her friends.

BESEECH: (v) To beg for with urgency
He beseeched his friend to help him get out of trouble with the coach.

COLLIDE: (v) To crash in motion
The two players collided on the field, knocking both of them down to the ground.

DOMINATE: (v) To command or control over
The team began to dominate in the game after falling behind and finally won.

DWELL: (v) To focus on something for a long time
She dwelled on the memories of her grandmother with fondness.

ENIGMA: (n) Something or someone puzzling or mysterious
Mathematical equations were a complete enigma to the creative writer.

LUMINOUS: (adj) Full of shining light
The room had been decorated with luminous candles that smelled like vanilla.

METICULOUS: (adj) Showing precise detail
Her meticulous way of accomplishing things made her a reliable person.

STATIONARY: (adj) Motionless, not meant to be moved
The stationary statue in the corner of the garden had vines creeping up it.

VIBRANT: (adj) Lively, full of enthusiasm, spirited
He had such a vibrant personality, everyone wanted to be his friend.

CREATIVE WRITING STARTER:

I did not dwell on the past; I only looked forward towards the future.
The luminous hope that burned vibrantly inside me dominated my every thought ...

PROMPT # 11

What if you found a genie in a bottle? What if that genie could grant you three wishes?
What if you couldn't ask for more wishes or undo one that turned disasterous?
Write a poem about what your **THREE WISHES** are and why they are important to you.

STYLE:
Rhyme Scheme: ababab cdcdcd efefef
Three Stanzas—one per wish

POETIC DEVICES:
Load this one up with Alliteration

PROMPT # 12

Now that you have created a poem about **THREE WISHES**,
write another poem in response to your three wishes and explain what happened
as if the wishes came true.
What were the **CONSEQUENCES**, good or bad, of each wish?

STYLE:
Rhyme Scheme: aabba ccddc eeffe
Three Stanzas—one per consequence of wish coming true

POETIC DEVICES:
Load this one up with Hyperboles

_____

_____

_____

_____

_____

_____

_____

_____

_____

_____

_____

_____

_____

_____

_____

_____

_____

_____

_____

_____

_____

_____

_____

_____

_____

_____

_____

_____

_____

_____

_____

_____

_____

_____

_____

_____

_____

_____

_____

WRITE

_____

_____

_____

_____

_____

_____

_____

_____

_____

_____

_____

_____

_____

_____

_____

_____

_____

_____

_____

_____

_____

WONDROUS WORDS

ADMONISH: (v) To warn or scold someone harshly
The teacher admonished the student for cheating on the test.

AUTHENTIC: (adj) Genuine, not copied or false
The Old World Map was authentic and worth millions of dollars.

CAPTIVATE: (v) To charm or attract the interest of
The bright, colorful lights captivated the viewers watching the display.

ENTHRALL: (v) Capture the attention of
The creepy music enthralled the people watching the scary show.

GAUDY: (adj) Detailed or having many elements
The decorations for the school dance were so gaudy no one could tell what the true theme was.

INTRICATE: (adj) Detailed or having many elements
The intricate details of the painting made it look like a photograph.

PIQUE: (v) To provoke one's curiosity
He had piqued the interest of the crowd with his amusing story.

STANCE: (n) A specific way someone stands
Her stance indicated that she was still angry about it.

SULLEN: (adj) In a bad mood
He was still sullen after losing the game.

YEARN: (v) A strong desire for something
She yearned for a chance at the lead role in the play.

CREATIVE WRITING STARTER:

Every aspect of the quest captivated and enthralled me.
I knew the treasure map was authentic, and I yearned to discover its gold ...

PROMPT # 13

Write a Haiku poem all about something or someone you enjoy.

STYLE:
Haiku
See page 124 for instructions
on how to write a Haiku,
as well as see several examples

TWIST:
Write to an imaginary audience, turning the Haiku into Free Verse poetry,
using lots of Imagery, Hyperboles, and a few Onomatopoeias.

PROMPT # 14

Write a poem about an INANIMATE OBJECT.
Describe it using as much Imagery as you can.
What does the object do? Why is the object of interest to you?
You can write the poem with one-liners,
describing each attribute of the object using sight, smell, sound, taste, and touch.
Then add Personification to the object so that it becomes humanlike.

TWIST:
Interact with the object as if it were alive, and you were having a conversation with it.
Do not say what the object is until the last line of your poem.

WRITE

WONDROUS WORDS

AGILE: (adj) able to move swiftly and easily
The athlete was <u>agile</u> on his feet on the court.

BANTER: (n) Playful, friendly exchange of conversation
Their <u>banter</u> was so easy they knew they would be friends forever.

CLAD: (adj) clothed
He was <u>clad</u> in a flannel shirt and jeans.

ESCALATE: (v) To increase quickly
After a while, the casual conversation <u>escalated</u> into a more serious talk.

NONCHALANT: (adj) Behaving calm and relaxed
He was so <u>nonchalant</u> about the crisis at hand, his friends were a little worried about him.

OVERWHELM: (v) To be engulfed or buried
The flood <u>overwhelmed</u> the homes, sending many to their rooftops.

PROWESS: (n) Mastering a skill, an expert
His <u>prowess</u> was in programming the coolest video games.

RUBBLE: (n) Debris or fragments from a building
After the recking ball leveled the building, the <u>rubble</u> was all that remained.

SERENE: (adj) Peaceful and calm
The sound of the rain was so <u>serene</u> that she almost fell asleep listening to it.

VOID: (adj) empty or vacant
The mysterious mansion at the end of the block was <u>void</u> of any decor and smelled of mold.

CREATIVE WRITING STARTER:

I wandered through the <u>rubble</u> <u>nonchalantly</u>, clad in boots and carrying a shovel,
not even the least bit <u>overwhelmed</u> by the amount of work I had to do ...

PROMPT # 15

What if you dwelled in the SEA or flew above in the SKY?
Which location would you choose? What creature would you be?
Imagine you could do both.
Write a poem about your experience.

STYLE:
Free Verse
Poetic Devices: Alliteration, Imagery, Simile

TWIST:
Write three poems—one for each experience.
Write one poem that includes both experiences and alternate SEA or SKY with each stanza.

PROMPT # 16

What if you had to relive the SAME DAY over and over again?
Write a poem about a day—good or bad—in which you had to do the same tasks
for three days in a row. You are able to change how you react to the same events, though.
Write a Narrative Free Verse Poem in which the first stanza describes what your day is like.
Then, for the second stanza and the third stanza,
change how you handle each day differently.

TWIST:
Try to make it Rhyme like a Dr. Seuss book.
Poetic Devices: Imagery, Personification, Hyperbole

_____

_____

_____

_____

_____

_____

_____

_____

_____

_____

_____

_____

_____

_____

_____

_____

_____

_____

WONDROUS WORDS

ASCEND: (v) To rise or climb up
She began to ascend the stairs to go to the upper family room.

DISTRESS: (n) Intense pain, anxiety, or sadness
The distress he was in after breaking his leg made him growl in agony.

EBULLIENT: (adj) Cheerful and energetic
Her ebullient attitude always kept her friends in the best of moods.

FEEBLE: (adj) Weak in strength especially due to age
His grandmom had become so feeble, he always let her lean on him when they went for walks.

HEARTY: (adj) Ample, filling, wholesome
She ate a hearty bowl of stew that had beef and potatoes in it.

LIKENESS: (n) Resemblance or similarity
Their likeness made others think they were related, but they were just friends.

MEAGER: (adj) Inadequate or limited in quality or quantity
The meager amount of work they had to do relieved them because they would be done quickly.

NIMBLE: (adj) Quick and acrobatic in movement
The athlete was so nimble, she practically flew over all the hurdles.

PREPOSTEROUS: (adj) Absurd, opposing common sense
His reasoning was so preposterous that the class erupted in laughter at his comment.

STRIDENT: (adj) Making a creaking or harsh sound
The strident crickets were so loud that they all had trouble sleeping that night.

CREATIVE WRITING STARTER:

There was no room for meager doubts in my mind and giving up was preposterous to me.
I had to escape the distress I was under and head towards safety with nimble moves ...

PROMPT # 17

Write an **AUTOBIOGRAPHICAL** poem that describes who you are and what you are all about.
What makes you unique? What makes you blend in? What were you like as a child?
How have you changed? Are there things about yourself you want to keep changing?
Who or what are some influences in your life that have helped shape you
into who you are today? What interests you? What disgusts you?
What have you accomplished so far, and do you have specific plans for your future?

TWIST:
Write this poem as an ABC Poem in which you start each line
with the letters of the English Alphabet, starting with A and ending with Z.
Add as many Similes and Metaphors as you can to describe yourself and your interests.

PROMPT # 18

TONGUE TWISTERS are a special kind of fun.
Meant to be spoken out loud, little poems tangle up speech by loading each line
with words that all start with the same letter and make the same sound. In other words,
Tongue Twisters are a practical exercise in using the poetic device: Alliteration.

Write several Tongue Twisters using Alliteration.
See if you can incorporate as many Onomatopoeias as you can in each line
to give the poem a lot of additional sound effects.

TWIST:
Write Tongue Twisters for all the letters in your first name.

WRITE

_____

_____

_____

_____

_____

_____

_____

_____

_____

_____

_____

_____

_____

_____

_____

_____

_____

_____

_____

Structured
Poetry

Hey? Psst! There's nothing wrong with shrugging at a blank page when you're all out of ideas and reverting to writing something you are familiar with structurally. Poetry comes in all shapes, sizes, and styles. Some people only write poems that are specific to a set of rules, and we don't mind if they do. Others prefer to free-style all their writing, and we simply get out of their way and let them do their thing. Thinking back to the pages I front-loaded you with at the beginning of this workbook, you'll remember that poems can rhyme if you want them to, or not. Poems can contain rigid metrical feet or even hop around with specifc syllabic counts per line, too. All poems have poetic devices in them, no matter what. Regardless, of your preferences when writing, I want you to try your hand at some oldy-but-goody styles. I decided to add a few structured poetry styles in this section that I think you are already familiar with like Haiku and Quatrains, but I added a couple other styles, as well, that you may not have ever heard of. I'd like to see you try to emulate these styles of poetry, if you're up for the challenge.

STRUCTURED POETRY

Haiku
Quatrain
Slam
Lyric
Cento
(with a twist)

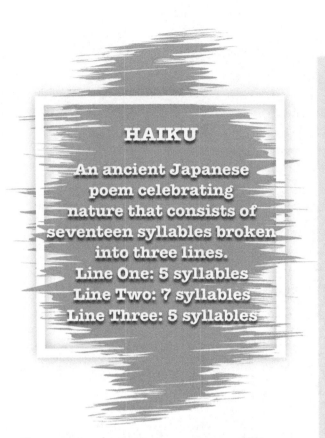

HAIKU

An ancient Japanese poem celebrating nature that consists of seventeen syllables broken into three lines.
Line One: 5 syllables
Line Two: 7 syllables
Line Three: 5 syllables

On upcoming pages, you will see examples written by me that break the 'no title' rule, as well as lists of one-liners to create Haiku with for practice in the brainstorming box available. I also included journal pages for you to experiment with using some of the themes I've listed below.

PROMPTS:

spring, summer, fall, winter
friendship, love, family
landscapes, locations
school, vacation, holidays
hobbies, sports, art, music
interests, skills, fears

Dear Writer,

You are probably all too familiar with writing Haiku poetry. If you didn't know its roots, though, Haiku began with Japanese poet, Matsuo Bashō. Bashō (1644-1694), during the Edo period in Japan, developed the Haiku as a spin-off on the first stanza of a Renga, known as a Hokku. Bashō polished the syllabic count into the Haiku we know today. With a total of seventeen syllables broken into three lines, the first containing five syllables, the second containing seven, and the third containing five more syllables, poets have been practicing their creativity writing Haiku since elementary school. Originally meant to celebrate nature, Haiku can be adapted to any theme the writer wishes to write about. Though, traditionally, Haiku poetry does not contain titles, I personally like to add them to my poems to create a punchline effect, as you'll see in the spread of examples I share with you.

~Brooke E. Wayne

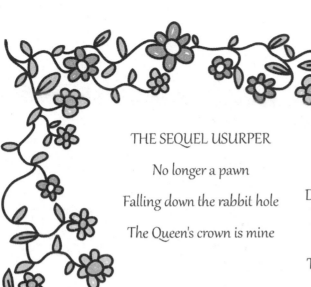

THE SEQUEL USURPER

No longer a pawn

Falling down the rabbit hole

The Queen's crown is mine

THE TIME CHANGE

Vanishing sunshine

Daylight no longer lingers

Winter closes in

THE INTROVERT

Shaken to my core

I rise above the chaos

Parting from the crowd

THE LAKE

Liquid silver stilled

An ancient rock skitters by

Shattering moonlight

THE RIVERBED SONG

Forest life wakes to

Babbling brook whispering

Across silken stones

THE INVISIBLE GIRL

Each tear an ocean

Drowning in heartache for you

Notice me just once

THE FRONT PORCH

That first sip of tea

As twilight cloaks me in peace

Warming me inside

THE VOWS

One passionate kiss

Proclaims promises to keep

Tangling two souls

THE BOND

Unbreakable trust

Binds us together as one

Forever in love

THE POWERHOUSE

Mitochondria

Breaking and rebuilding life

Journey into cells

Haiku Poetry by Brooke E. Wayne

5 SYLLABLE ONE-LINERS

dew kissed spiderweb
mist covered mountain
timeless memories
dark hopes awaken
cold twilight sea breeze
shimmering starlight

7 SYLLABLE ONE-LINERS

inspiring thoughts of day
presses against the front door
on a dim and weathered trail
casting cold, moonlit shadows
memories flash in my mind
awakening calm waters
fireflies glow so brightly

5 SYLLABLE ONE-LINERS

with a hopeful praise
promises held true
in a quiet hush
on this gentle lake
on the journey there
when the sun will set
Winter celebrates

_____

_____

_____

_____

_____

_____

_____

_____

_____

_____

_____

_____

_____

_____

_____

_____

_____

_____

_____

_____

_____

_____

_____

_____

_____

_____

_____

_____

_____

_____

_____

_____

_____

_____

_____

_____

_____

_____

_____

_____

_____

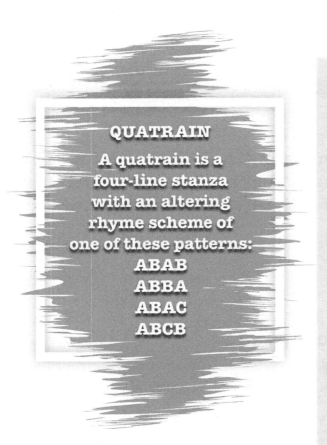

QUATRAIN

A quatrain is a four-line stanza with an altering rhyme scheme of one of these patterns:
ABAB
ABBA
ABAC
ABCB

On the following pages, you will see a fill-in poem for you to practice composing a creative writing piece that utilizes several Quatrains. Finish the example poem, then proceed to write all the Quatrains your heart desires on the journal pages. I have even added a brainstorming box for you to write some rhyming sets of words in to build your Quatrains around.

Dear Writer,

I need to start out the explanation of what a Quatrain is by first addressing its predecessor, the Couplet. By definition, a Couplet is as simple as its name. It's a couple of lines. They rhyme together. That's all.

Quatrains, on the other hand, have four lines that contain rhymes and can be presented in different patterns. As long as there is a rhyme scheme where the ends of the lines rhyme together in one of the given alternating patterns, then you have a Quatrain.

This type of poem is also the foundational structure of building more lengthy poems by turning Quatrains into stanzas and adding as many as you want to make a--you guessed it--bigger poem. Think of Quatrains as stanzas in a poem the way paragraphs make up an essay. Lots of quatrains can create a different type of poem. Several other structured poems use couplets, quatrains, and other small groupings of lines to make Sonnets, Villanelles, and so on.

~Brooke E. Wayne

QUATRAIN
FILL-IN

Directions: Finish this poem by completing the Quatrain below that has an AABB Rhyme Scheme pattern. You could also say it's a poem composed of couplets, too, because of the given Rhyme Scheme.

An End to Loneliness

(A)   With a heart of <u>stone</u>
(A)   He only wanted to be <u>alone</u>
(B)   But the wandering dog wouldn't go <u>away</u>
(B)   So the old man just let it <u>stay</u>

(C)   _____
(C)   _____
(D)   _____
(D)   _____

(E)   _____
(E)   _____
(F)   _____
(F)   _____

On the following pages, write more Quatrain poetry using the other Rhyme Scheme patterns of ABAB, ABCB, and ABBA.

_____

_____

_____

_____

_____

_____

_____

_____

_____

_____

_____

_____

_____

_____

_____

_____

_____

_____

_____

_____

_____

_____

_____

_____

_____

_____

_____

_____

_____

_____

_____

_____

_____

_____

_____

_____

_____

_____

_____

_____

_____

_____

_____

_____

_____

_____

_____

_____

_____

_____

_____

_____

_____

_____

_____

_____

_____

_____

_____

_____

SLAM

Slam poetry is a performance art in a competitive setting. Poems are delivered in front of a participating audience. Slam poetry is often personal and highly emotional.

Slam Jam competitions thrive on the audience's reaction dictating who the winner is. Poems, therefore, tend to come from the heart and soul of the poet.
Popular themes include:
Personal Struggles
Personal Victories
Finding Oneself
Political Stances
Cultural Topics
Social Disparities
Economic Statuses
Meaningful Relationships
The Speaker's Passion

Dear Writer,

Poetry comes in all kinds of forms, not just as a written expression of one's heart and soul, but as spoken words, too. Slam poetry is a unique kind of poetry as a performing art. A slam poem is meant to be delivered in front of a participating audience in a competitive nature with other fellow Slam poets.

The poem is expressed on stage with all the bells and whistles of body language, as no props, music, or lighting effects are allowed to enhance the recitation. The poem is meant to be a personal expression, although, a Slam poem can be presented by more than a single speaker.

The audience dictates the 'winner' of the competition based on the most receptive response, while each poet has three minutes or less to 'upstage' the other performers in the competition.

YouTube is full of Slam Jam clips, if you're interested in seeing one. Just like a written poem, Slam poetry is loaded with poetic devices. The only difference is, because it is spoken, tone and voice is everything.

Be sure to read your Slam poems out loud after you write them!

~Brooke E. Wayne

SLAM JAM

My Teacher

My teacher WOKE me
  made me see my own TRUTH

    She took me from a place of sweet solace
      stole me to my FEARS

        I walk ALONE
          I RUN with her
            A WOMAN, she'll make me be

Do it RIGHT
  Be your BEST
    FORGIVE, FORGET
      MOVE ON, she'd say

      My teacher made me LEARN it all
        I get NO BREAKS in life, all STRIFE

Be STRONG
  Be BRAVE
    Be YOURSELF
  Learn to WALK AWAY, she'd say

      My teacher is my ROCK, my ROOTS
        my grinding stone, sharpening my WORDS, my MIND

        Nothing but LOVE I LIVE and BREATHE now
        That's the truth I now SEE

My teacher is my EVERYTHING
  my FLESH
    my BLOOD
      my MOTHER

She is half of ME

by
Brooke E. Wayne

LYRIC
Expresses intense
emotions, capturing
a moment in time.
Often lyric poetry
is accompanied by
musical instruments
and sung.
Songs are composed
of lyrics.

If you want to put poetic devices that you are good at creating into your Lyric poetry, then do it. No one is saying you can't. Just remember to pour a little heart into the words while you're at it. Lyric poetry is often written from a first-person point-of-view and tends to rhyme, creating a natural, musical effect. For that reason, Lyric poetry often works well to accompany music, though, but no pressure.
Pro Tip: Listen to some music while you're writing some Lyric poetry.
It will do wonders for inspiration.

Dear Writer,
    It doesn't take a genius to figure out that Lyric poetry is the stuff songs are made of. Song lyrics are every bit poetry--Lyric poetry to be exact. Not every Lyric poem is going to have lots of obvious poetic devices in it, though. Since the nature of this type of poem is to express strong emotions, the use of imagery is often left behind. You might not find any similes or metaphors in them either. That's not to say the poet can't add them if he or she wishes to, it's just, when dealing with matters of the heart, as this type of poem focuses on, the lines tend to revolve around feelings of the intangible kind. Lyric poetry tends to focus on creating a distinct mood for the reader.
    Not all Lyric poetry is meant to be performed, though. Yes, all songs are composed of Lyrics, but not all poetry of a lyrical nature should be translated into a song. Not everyone can sing nor play musical intruments, so don't think that writing Lyric poetry is not for you if you can't turn your work into a musical hit.

~Brooke E. Wayne

LYRIC FILL-IN

Directions: Complete the rest of the stanzas in the Lyric Poem below. Then write additional Lyrical Poetry on the journal pages provided.

The Independent

(A)   I've never been a realist
(B)   Always sticking my head in the clouds
(C)   Just want to do my own thing
(B)   I'm not one to follow crowds

(D)   _____
(E)   _____
(F)   _____
(E)   _____

(G)   _____
(H)   _____
(I)   _____
(H)   _____

(J)   _____
(J)   _____

Possible Themes: Interests, Hobbies, Sports, Television Series, Movies, Songs, Bands, Singers, Favorites, Not-So-Favorites, Friendship, Enemies, Family, School, Skills, Talents, Arts, Habits

_____

_____

_____

_____

_____

_____

_____

_____

_____

_____

_____

_____

_____

_____

_____

_____

_____

_____

_____

_____

WRITE

_____

_____

_____

_____

_____

_____

_____

_____

_____

_____

_____

_____

_____

_____

_____

_____

_____

_____

_____

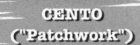

CENTO
("Patchwork")

A Cento poem borrows
singular lines
from famous poems,
knitting together an
original poem.
Traditionally,
each line must come from
a different poet.

Traditionally, Cento poems are composed of lines from different poems. For a **CENTO WITH A TWIST,** I want you to compose one using lines from your favorite songs.

ALTERNATE CENTO THEMES:

SONG TITLES
OPENING LINES OF NOVELS
LAST LINES OF NOVELS
QUOTES FROM NOVELS
PRODUCT SLOGANS
MULTICULTURAL PROVERBS

Fill up the journal pages with your **CENTO WITH A TWIST,** as well as a traditional Cento, or use one of the alternate suggestions above.

Dear Writer,

A CENTO literally means "patchwork", like quilting squares pieced together to create a singular blanket. Traditionally, a CENTO is composed of one-liners from different poets that would then have attributes at the end of the poem, giving credit where credit is due.

I want you to think about your favorite songs. Search up their lyrics, and write down several of them from various musicians. Then string the lines together so that they compose a poem that makes sense to you. Be sure to put a note at the end of the poem, honoring who wrote or sang each line.

You could also take lines from several songs sung by a singular musician or band and compose your CENTO that way, too. Regardless of how you choose to create your CENTO WITH A TWIST, take pleasure in the research of all those Lyric poems set to music. See if you can find any poetic devices hidden among the words while you're at it.

~Brooke E. Wayne

EXAMPLE OF ORIGINAL CENTO:

Everything Carries Me to You

You are violets with wind above them
  And shreds of shadowy laughter
    That looks on tempests and is never shaken.
One kind glance from thine eye,
  In which the Heart is caught,
    And I'll forget the past!
For One must wait
  To find if hearts be wild and wise ...
So long as the world contains us both,
  Love's web is spun.

Brooke E. Wayne

Attributes:
(Title--Pablo Neruda, "If You Forget Me")
(Line 1--Ezra Pound, "A Girl")
(Line 2--Rupert Brooke, "Beauty and Beauty")
(Line 3--William Shakespeare, "Sonnet 116")
(Line 4--Charlotte Brontë, "Passion")
(Line 5--Emily Dickinson, "Escape is such a thankful Word")
(Line 6--Jane Austen, "Oh! Mr. Best You're Very Bad")
(Line 7--Emily Dickinson, "I cannot live with You")
(Line 8--William Butler Yeats, "The Mask")
(Line 9--Robert Browning, "Life in a Love")
(Line 10--Oscar Wilde, "Her Voice")

_____

_____

_____

_____

_____

_____

_____

_____

_____

_____

_____

_____

_____

_____

_____

_____

_____

_____

_____

_____

_____

_____

_____

_____

_____

_____

_____

_____

_____

_____

_____

_____

_____

_____

_____

_____

_____

_____

_____

_____

_____

_____

Pictorial Inspiration

Hey? Psst! I just want you to know,
before you dive headfirst into
the final exercise, I've enjoyed every step
of this adventure with you.
I am proud to have been cheering you on
as you've developed
some incredibly talented poems.
If words were musical notes,
I think we just created a symphonic
masterpiece, don't you?
As you go into the next writing challenge,
remember you can find inspiration
anywhere you look, any place you listen,
even among things that feel a certain way,
or move you to find your voice.
In the next section,
you'll see several pictures that are meant
to evoke an emotional response.
Choose a few of these captured moments to
write a poem about.
Be sure to add some poetic devices,
and play around with a rhyme scheme
or two, as well.
Until we write together again ...

PICTORIAL INSPIRATION

Directions: Pick a few pictures that inspire you to write. Then compose a poem for each of them, using all the "tricks" you've been taught. Write Free-Verse poems or create a whimsical Rhyme Scheme, if you feel inspired to do so.

_____

_____

_____

_____

_____

_____

_____

_____

_____

_____

_____

_____

_____

_____

_____

_____

_____

_____

_____

_____

_____

_____

_____

_____

_____

_____

_____

_____

_____

_____

_____

_____

_____

_____

_____

_____

_____

_____

_____

_____

_____

_____

_____

_____

_____

_____

_____

_____

_____

_____

_____

_____

_____

_____

_____

_____

_____

_____

_____

_____

_____

_____

_____

_____

_____

_____

_____

_____

_____

_____

_____

_____

_____

_____

_____

_____

_____

_____

_____

_____

_____

_____

_____

_____

_____

WRITE

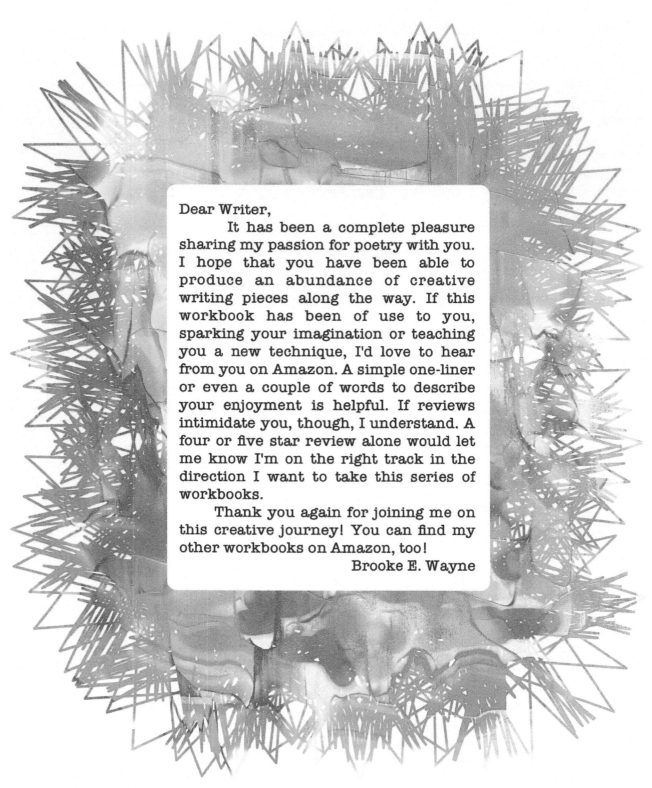

Dear Writer,

It has been a complete pleasure sharing my passion for poetry with you. I hope that you have been able to produce an abundance of creative writing pieces along the way. If this workbook has been of use to you, sparking your imagination or teaching you a new technique, I'd love to hear from you on Amazon. A simple one-liner or even a couple of words to describe your enjoyment is helpful. If reviews intimidate you, though, I understand. A four or five star review alone would let me know I'm on the right track in the direction I want to take this series of workbooks.

Thank you again for joining me on this creative journey! You can find my other workbooks on Amazon, too!

Brooke E. Wayne

How to Write a Review:

Sign into your Amazon Account, go to Orders, and Click on "Write a Product Review" on the right.

BROOKE E. WAYNE is a Romantic Comedy author who lives the RomCom dream in California. She is married to South Philly-born, Eagles-obsessed YouTuber Philly.500, who she met online and fell in love with long before that kind of meet cute was cool. They have two young daughters who flood their happily-ever-after lives with girly giggles and immeasurable love.

She holds a BA in English with a minor in Theology, a MA in Humanities with an emphasis in Literature, two Clear CLAD credentials, and an unofficial PhD in the Art of Snark.

Never without a journal on hand, Brooke has been writing stories and poetry since she was eleven years old. She's had everything from poetry to articles for an encyclopedia set published over the last thirty years. Her romance novels are available on Amazon.

When she is not crafting sensual, contemporary romances with light-hearted, witty twists, she teaches English Language Arts, inspiring others to read classic literature and write from the heart.

Brooke E. Wayne

Romance with a Kiss of Humor

Website: http://www.brookeewayne.com
Facebook Page: https://www.facebook.com/brookeewayne
Instagram: https://www.instagram.com/authorbrookeewayne
Twitter: https://www.twitter.com/brookeewayne
Bookbub: https://www.bookbub.com/profile/brooke-e-wayne
Pinterest: http://www.pinterest.com/authorbrookeewayne

Publications by Brooke E. Wayne:

CREATIVE WRITING WORKBOOKS

◆Adults & Teens ◆Tweens & Young Teens ◆Children

◆Poetic Devices ◆Examples ◆Starter Prompts ◆Fill-in-the-Blanks ◆Vocabulary
◆Interactive Experiences ◆Picture Prompts ◆Structured Poems ◆Tips & Tricks

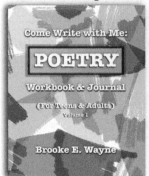 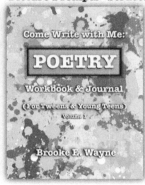 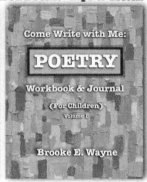

ROMANTIC COMEDY NOVELS

Whine with Cheese (Romantic Comedy Novel)
Love the Wine You're With (Romantic Comedy Novel)
COMING SOON! Wine Not? (Romantic Comedy Novel)

Made in the USA
Las Vegas, NV
16 April 2022